T0209783

LEADERSHIP
INSIGHTS

Tips To Learn, Grow, and Transform

M. W. Kublin and J. Mayer-Rodriguez

authorHOUSE®

AuthorHouse™
1663 Liberty Drive
Bloomington, IN 47403
www.authorhouse.com
Phone: 1 (800) 839-8640

Published by AuthorHouse 11/11/2019

ISBN: 978-1-7283-3212-3 (sc)
ISBN: 978-1-7283-3211-6 (e)

Library of Congress Control Number: 2019916751

Print information available on the last page.

This book is printed on acid-free paper.

Table of Contents

Dedication

To all leaders that understand learning is a process, not an event, and that a commitment for continual learning is a must for both new and seasoned leaders.

Introduction

A key piece of effective leadership is having a strong sense of awareness, both of self and of others. Do you know your strengths and weaknesses? Do you know that over-using a strength may result in a weakness?

How well do you interact with others? Are you in tune with their styles and preferences and do you have the ability to draw out and leverage their unique talents to strengthen the workplace?

Our 52 tips are meant to increase these levels by building and refreshing leadership skills, behaviors, and habits. We recommend reviewing and sharing one tip each week. Reflect on the message, assess what you could do differently to become more effective, and challenge your colleagues, team, and organization to do the same.

Are you ready to learn, grow, and transform?

Author's Note

I am so proud of our PeopleTek Team. For 20+ years we've been helping individuals of all levels succeed and be less frustrated and more effective in their roles as leaders. We believe that everyone is a leader regardless of title, role or level, as we all have the ability to influence others.

The sooner each of us has the courage to deal with the daily adversity we face in our jobs, and with our bosses, customers and colleagues, the better it is for everyone.

Our coaching team has helped so many individuals and teams increase their awareness levels and address the obstacles that were holding them back. It also lends itself to the practice of living our professional vision, mission and goals that will transform any team and culture.

We've been providing weekly leadership tips for over a decade, and I receive feedback everywhere I go that our tips help leaders practice their skills, abilities and talents each day in the workplace.

This makes my heart sing because we will now have healthier leaders, teams and organizations that stop practicing toxic behaviors and start coaching to innovation, growth and prosperity for all. Let's all practice together!

Sincerely,
Mike

Tip 1

Top Leadership Challenges

When leaders are doing their best, they Model the Way, Inspire a Shared Vision, Challenge the Process, Enable Others to Act, and Encourage the Heart—James M. Kouzes

Many studies have been conducted about leadership challenges, and most have quite a few commonalities:

- Developing effective leadership skills
- Managing through change
- Consistently recognizing and rewarding accomplishments
- Inspiring others
- Clearly communicating Vision, Mission and Goals and how they can, and must be, supported
- Building trust within teams and across organizations
- Being aware of, and having the skills, to address conflict

That's a relatively short list. Which do you find most troublesome? Which challenges would you add?

As leaders, we need to be self aware. How do we see ourselves? How do we show-up? Next is the tough part, how do others see us? Answering these questions may add to our personal list of challenges.

To SELF ASSESS, ask yourself:

1. *What's the purpose of my leadership?*
2. *Would my staff feel that I'm committed to their improvement?*
3. *Do I feel I make a real difference and feel valued? Would my staff agree?*
4. *Do I create and maintain relationships that help the organization thrive and obtain results?*
5. *Do I know what's expected of me and do I deliver on those expectations?*
6. *Do others know what I expect of them?*
7. *Are my priorities clearly communicated and supported?*
8. *Do I take sufficient action to improve individual and team performance?*
9. *Am I committed to self development?*
10. *Is going to work enjoyable? (at least most of the time?)*
11. *What keeps me up at night?*
12. *What are my challenges and what am I doing to address them?*

Being a leader is not easy and requires courage. Did you discover anything new from the assessment?

Name at least one leadership challenge you'll begin to develop, starting today!

_____

Tip 2

Having A Clear Vision

*A vision without a task is but a dream, a
task without a vision is drudgery, a vision
and a task is the hope of the world.*—
Church Of Sussex England, 1750

Plain and simple – in order for there to be organizational success, a clear **vision** must exist.

We have an equation: VMGM=B. It means that our vision, mission, goals and measures are to be 100% supported by our behaviors.

We define **Vision** as:

A *dream or aspiration* that provides *direction* and guides us to a place far away. It may be unattainable, but we are able to focus our attention and make strides for ideally getting there.

The idea is for the vision to be clearly defined, easily understood, with supporting actions made a priority. And, the entire organization (all levels; all positions) must be engaged.

This isn't always easy and things sometimes get derailed – how can each person and every role support it? That's where leadership comes in.

As leaders:

- We need to simplify the vision and make the connections for our staff/teams
- We need to regularly restate the vision and associated goals that will make the vision come alive
- We need to explain the "why" and obtain buy-in for the "how"
- We can also ask our team members their thoughts about making the vision feel real and meaningful to them
- We need to track and share any team successes and accomplishments that support the vision (and celebrate them!)

There is no right or wrong vision statement as long as it's a dream or aspiration that provides direction.

Do you have a documented (and communicated) vision statement?

Is it understood and shared across the workplace?

What have you done to make it come alive?

Tip 3

Mission Statements and Goals

*Outstanding people have one thing
in common: An absolute sense
of mission.*—Zig Ziglar

Mission statements bring clarity to our vision; it represents what we must do to support realizing our vision, and it personalizes it for us.

Here are some tips to help you define your vision statement and supporting goals:

#1. What services do you offer? What differentiates you from your competition?

#2. Who is or could be your customer? Describe an ideal customer.

#3. From your customer's viewpoint, what do they want?

#4. Why will the customers buy your product or service? What value and/or unique service are provided to the customer?

#5. You must assess the intent of your business or organization. Is it:

Customer focused? Customer Intimacy focuses on the needs of the customer and building relationships and is usually higher cost/less volume.

Operations focused? Operations Excellence focuses on the process and is volume driven and is usually low cost/high volume.

Product focused? Product Innovative focuses on the product. Expenses are geared towards research and development.

#6. What accomplishments would you like to celebrate this year? Next year? What targets will you aim for? ex. financial, marketing and sales, staff, operations, human resources, engineering, R&D, other.

If your team members were asked what their mission statement was, and for the 3 top goals they needed to support this year, would they be able to answer "yes" and list them?

Ask them!

Tip 4

Purposeful Behaviors

*The ABC's are attitude, behavior and
communication skills.*—Gerald Chertavian

As leaders it's essential that we are purposeful with our
behaviors, and all of our behaviors must support the
achievement of our vision, mission, and goals (VMG).

This obviously requires that we are intimately aware of our
VMG, that we are not only very clear in our role, but that
we have a deeper understanding of HOW our role impacts
successfully living and achieving our VMG.

As Plato says: *BEHAVIOR flows from our desire, emotion,
and knowledge.*

We also have to ensure our key processes and strategies are
linked with our vision, mission and goals. This includes:

- Hiring
- Training and development
- Performance Appraisals
- Rewards and Recognition
- Communication plans (the mode, the frequency, the level of content)
- Change (anything new?)
- Conflict (managing differences and expectations)

Do you want your behaviors to be modeled by others? Be honest! Ideally we'll see positive behaviors in others, and if we're truly effective leaders, some of those behaviors we observe may have been influenced by our own actions.

You know the old clichés:

Walk the talk. Practice what you preach. Lead by example. Actions speak louder than words. Don't ask others to do something you're not willing to do. Be continual learners. Practice and apply new learnings. Be open to feedback. Listen twice as much as you talk.

Bottom line: be aware that we as leaders are indeed observed so model the behaviors that will help us, our colleagues, and our direct reports achieve the vision, mission, and goals for our organization.

Have you observed your positive behaviors in others?

Do you look for positive behaviors in others that you can model?

Tip 5

What's Magic Dust™?

*Everyone has a purpose in life and a unique
talent to give to others. And when we blend
this unique talent with service to others,
we experience the ecstasy and exultation
of own spirit, which is the ultimate goal
of all goals.*—Kallam Anji Reddy

Have you ever heard the term "Magic Dust"™? Unless you've worked with PeopleTek, the answer is likely no. We coined the term and define it as:

- What you're good at
- Your unique skills and abilities
- Qualities that make you more impactful
- How and where you add the most value

Ideally we are provided opportunities to leverage our special skills and abilities at work, allowing us to add the most value, to find our work fulfilling, and best yet, feel inspired and invigorated!

Each of us in general are pretty good at assessing and scrutinizing what we don't like doing. We know what we are not good at, but we're not always clear on what makes us have a great day, or provides us with a sense of accomplishment and generally feeling good.

How would you define a good work day? Does it include leading others or contributing to their success? This is part of being a leader. Leadership can be formal (ex. direct reports, matrix management, project manager, mentorships, etc), or it could be informal, where your skills lend themselves to you taking "charge". This frequently includes using your skills and abilities to build relationships, achieve common goals and objectives, assist others with your technical savvy, or maybe even simply listening.

What leadership qualities do you bring to your team or organization? Are you able to integrate your gifts/strengths both in your career and in your personal life? It's great when your ambition and talents serve you rather than enslave you!

This may sound funny, but we have worked with leaders that excel at what they do, are acknowledged, appreciated, and rewarded for their accomplishments, but they quite simply don't LIKE what they're doing!

Hopefully that does not apply to you. Knowing and using your gifts and skills will energize you and increase your level of fulfillment, and sharing them with others will add to your sense of purpose.

- Where do you feel you add the most value?
- Where would others say you provide the greatest value?
- Are you able to identify the Magic Dust™ of your colleagues?

Tip 6

Trust In The Workplace

*Transparency, honesty, and vulnerability
are the key ingredients required
for a team to be trusting and truly
cohesive.*—Patrick Lencioni

How would you rate trust within your organization? Are team members comfortable:

- *Admitting and owning weaknesses and mistakes?*
- *Asking for help?*
- *Offering and accepting apologies without hesitation?*
- *Sharing their knowledge to help others grow?*
- *Supporting shared goals where the team will be recognized as a team, rather than as individuals?*

Trust issues continually score high as a "need" for individuals, teams, and organizations. This pertains to relationships with colleagues, peers, and bosses, and can also apply to strategic partners and vendors.

Here are some tips for increasing trust:

- Assess whether there are any reasons others may not trust *you*. Work on them!
- Do you consistently display the behaviors you wish to see in others?
- How is your current work culture? What changes could be made to make it stronger?
- Select a highly trusted leader; identify the behaviors you feel make then successful and add them to your "tool-belt".
- ASK your team for their ideas about improving trust.
- Listen and be responsive!

What actions can you implement to improve trust in your workplace?

Does anyone come to mind that could benefit from your assistance with increasing levels of trust?

Tip 7

The Cost Of Conflict

For good ideas and true innovation,
you need human interaction, conflict,
argument, debate.—Margaret Heffernan

Conflict is positive when differences are discussed in a healthy manner but can be devastating when the conflict occurs with ill intentions.

Based on studies published by the *Washington Business Journal*, strained relationships account for 60-80% of conflict in the workplace, and managers typically spend 25 - 40% of their time dealing with conflict. That equates to 1-2 days every workweek!

And, the cost of workplace conflict in the U.S. is estimated at **$359 Billion annually** (2.8 hours per week @ $17.95 per hour).

When many people hear the word "conflict" they think of negative situations. It may be, or in its simplest form, it means a disagreement or difference of opinion which can be inspirational and lend itself to creativity and growth. Problems arise when differences are not managed, ill feelings surface, morale diminishes, and productivity suffers.

It's up to us as leaders to understand how we respond to conflict. We need to increase our awareness of not only our own conflict behaviors, but also those of our colleagues. And most importantly, we need to recognize destructive responses and replace them with productive ones.

An effective leader understands effective conflict management and when and how to get engaged.

They:

- Recognize that disputes can't be avoided
- Promptly address unproductive behaviors
- They mediate as needed and they listen to opposing points of view
- Promote a culture of awareness and understanding, and utilize assessments and coaching to promote team collaboration

Don't allow the conflicts in your workplace to impact productivity; instead, use them to inspire creativity, build stronger relationships, and improve the bottom line.

Conflict management requires skills – how well do you manage differences? How could you become more effective?

Tip 8

Did You Hear Me?

*To effectively communicate, we must
realize that we are all different in the
way we perceive the world and use
this understanding as a guide to our
communication with others.*—Tony Robbins

Hearing versus Listening. Do you consider them to mean the same thing? We're here to share how and why they are very different.

We hear things without any effort or thought. In reality, most of us have the ability to tune out what we view as distractions or if we view the information as inconsequential. Listening on the other hand requires focus, and in general includes being attentive to what is being said and processing the message with the intent to understand (and in most cases show that we're interested).

It's been reported that words represent only 7% of what we "hear", that volume, pitch, rhythm, and tone account for 38%, and that facial and body language represents 55%. No wonder it takes energy (and focus) to be an active listener.

Below are some reminders for improving our listening skills:

- No interrupting
- No multi-tasking
- Be aware of body language, expressions, and tone
- Listen for underlying meanings
- Be open to differing views
- Retain eye contact (this helps with attention levels)
- Don't suggest words or finish sentences when a pause occurs
- Don't solve or judge
- Ask probing questions to obtain clarity and recap what you think you've heard

Something else to be aware of is "selective" listening. Are there individuals that you seem to always be fully engaged with and others that you have the inclination to "tune out"? Does the "deliverers" age, skill, gender, title, or general demeanor affect your ability (and desire) to be an active listener? What else de-rails your ability to listen?

Awareness is key. Pay attention to your "non" listening behaviors ex. pencil tapping, raised eyebrows, blank stares, "zoning" out, making shopping lists, etc. If you have a "history" of losing focus with a particular person, make an extra effort to be attentive.

What can you do to be a more active listener?

Tip 9

Saying "NO" Is An Art

*The art of leadership is saying no, not saying
yes. It is very easy to say yes.*—Tony Blair

Saying "no" is difficult for many of us, but this simple word
must be incorporated into our vocabulary. We need to
understand why it's difficult for us, and the ramifications
for our reluctance.

We all want to succeed, our pace never slows down, we know
we can juggle and accomplish amazing things, and because
of this, we're sometimes guilty of over committing.

That's when we need to remember that saying NO is an
option (and an art!).

Things to think about:

- If we say "yes", what tasks will be negatively impacted?
- Are we compromising our ability to deliver quality work?
- How many additional hours are we willing to add to our schedule?
- Does the task clearly support our goals and priorities?
- We also have the option to counter-offer: *I'd love to support that initiative; I may need help assessing what could be reassigned elsewhere or postponed.*

Other tips:

- Have a plan in place to handle distractions and interruptions
- Know how to prioritize, be willing to re-prioritize, and commit to your decisions
- Set boundaries based on your priorities and say no to those outside your boundaries
- Be open and flexible, but realistic
- Practice the ways in which you can respond.

Be true to yourself and your priorities, and don't compromise quality. Remember that **over-using a strength** (our desire to achieve), could result in a weakness. (And it's likely to create self-imposed stress!).

Tip 10

Aware Or Out Of Touch?

Awareness is the ability to perceive,
to feel, or to be conscious of events,
objects, thoughts, emotions, or sensory
patterns . . . it is the state or quality of
being aware of something.—Wikipedia

We've already talked about developing skills in others; now we'll discuss developing ourselves. If someone asked you what your greatest skill or trait was, how would you respond?

Here are some things to consider:

- ✓ What do you do that adds the greatest value?
- ✓ What is your "magic dust™"?
- ✓ What differentiates you from your colleagues?
- ✓ How sharp are your technical skills?
- ✓ Do you hone your skills as change occurs?

- ✓ How do you contribute to making your team strong and whole?
- ✓ How do you strengthen business partner relationships?
- ✓ Are you a mentor or do you have a mentor?
- ✓ Do you know what motivates you?
- ✓ What type of task or assignment excites you?
- ✓ What type of task or assignment do you resist?
- ✓ What does your feedback tell you about becoming stronger?

We don't always take the necessary time to assess our skills and contributions. We may have been strong in our prior position, but are we doing all that we can to better enable us for career advancement?

Some think that development is the responsibility of their company. Why limit it to that? In today's economy we need to keep our skills sharp. After all, we were all initially hired based on our skill set; it's up to us to remain marketable and have a competitive edge. Invest in yourself. Know what makes you a key contributor and keep those skills strong; simultaneously identify two things that need strengthening and begin now!

Tip 11

BAM! You're A Leader

*Leadership is only courage and wisdom, and
a great carefulness of self.*—John Buchan

Many of us were promoted into leadership positions because
we were great at what we did. We excelled in our role, we
executed tasks with precision, and we met or exceeded goals
and deliverables.

All of a sudden "BAM"; you've become a leader with direct
reports and are not sure what all is involved. It doesn't matter
that you're unclear on what's required in your new role, or
that your "people" skills needed to be developed, refined
and/or refreshed. Sound familiar?

Some of us have had the opportunity to have a mentor and
be afforded career development opportunities. Some of us
have not had a smooth transition into our new leadership
role, and quite honestly have difficulty moving forward.

The good news is that we can help ourselves by learning new tools, and acquiring techniques and methods that are considered to be essential for leadership effectiveness.

This can be humbling, and it takes courage for successful professionals and technicians to admit they have gaps to fill.

A good starting point is to increase awareness levels; what's working well, what is not, what skill-sets need to be updated, and are customer/client needs being met? We have a complimentary self-assessment that we think you'll find helpful.

You (confidentially) rate yourself in the areas of **Awareness, Magic Dust, VMGM = B, Communication, Clarity, Accountability, Conflict, Influence, Relationships, Feedback, Inspiration, and Continual Learning.** (The assessment may be found at the back of the book).

After scoring yourself on a ten-point scale (from poor to superb), you will document your strengths and target development areas, and provide names for those you feel can provide you with developmental assistance. It will conclude with you determining "next steps" and timings.

Leadership development requires courage and commitment – and, it's a process not an event. (We know; you've heard this before. Numerous times!)

Why not utilize this leadership roadmap to update your development plan? Take your first step towards courageous leadership today!

Tip 12

Leading Remotely

*Leadership has challenges, and
it becomes even more challenging
when leading from a distance.*

Leadership has taken on new challenges with the need to lead
not only those that are in the same location, but to also be
effective across time zones, understand cultural differences,
and keep telecommuters engaged and productive.

Per GlobalWorkplaceAnalystics/2017:

- Regular telecommuting grew 115% in the past
  decade
- 70% of employers offer flexible workplace options
- 50% of the US workforce holds a job with at least
  partial telework

What does this mean to you as a leader?

As a leader, regardless of where your staff is located, make certain that common goals are clearly understood, encourage your team to value one another's strengths, and provide one another other with healthy, timely feedback.

Leading remotely also means you need to be an even more skilled communicator. Don't communicate just the bare minimum.

- Share what is expected of each individual and each location.
- Ensure all interactions end with closure.
- Check in regularly with each employee.
- Revisit the team goals and objectives; use "here's where we are" statements, ask questions, and invite everyone to share their opinion and thoughts about the progress that is being made.
- Ask your direct reports what they'd like to hear about and ask for their feedback as to whether you are keeping them adequately informed.
- Support and "sell" your team! Keep your boss and other leaders informed of your teams' accomplishments and successes!
- Look for opportunities for the team to meet face-to-face.

It takes effort for remote team members to feel as much a part of your team as those that work onsite but the tips above will help.

Tip 13

Passion=Energy

*Passion is energy. Feel the power
that comes from focusing on what
excites you.*—Oprah Winfrey

We talk about passion a lot; what we enjoy doing, what we do well, what comes easy to us, what behaviors/actions we get most recognized for. We call this our "Magic Dust"™.

When you're doing something you **like** or **want** to do, does your energy level increase? Ours does!

Things that increase energy levels include:

- Problem resolution
- Creative/innovative thinking
- Technical advancements
- Customer/client interactions
- Team building

- Developing the skill sets in others
- Providing feedback; mentorships
- Enhancing relationships
- Driving results
- Cost savings
- Meeting goals/completing tasks
- Quality deliverables; process improvements

In most situations, time seems to fly by when you're engaged in an activity you enjoy doing. We need however to be realistic; rarely can all of our time be dedicated to our passion. (Even when you're self employed there are tasks that MUST be done, despite feeling like drudgery).

- What are you passionate about at work?
- What brings you enjoyment? Can this be incorporated to a greater extent in your current position?
- Create a plan, talk to your boss, and make a case for how the organization/business will benefit if your role (or the roles of your direct reports) change.

Tip 14

First Lead Yourself

Your leadership depends on you. You can only be a great leader when you can lead yourself well first.—Richard Norris

We have a slogan: *FIRST LEAD YOURSELF (FLY), THEN LEAD OTHERS.*

What does this mean? Basically, as leaders we must understand what successful and effective leadership is comprised of. Next, we need to commit to developing our skills so that we possess those traits, behaviors, and skill-sets.

We'll break it down into five "C's":

CLARITY

This requires the absence of ambiguity in formulating where it is you're going and your plan for getting there

COMMUNICATION

Consistently and constantly sharing your vision, mission, and goals

COACHING

How could you be coached to be more effective?

COURAGE

Sticking to your vision regardless of external influences

COMMITMENT

It's being accountable and taking ownership of ALL your actions and behaviors

Once you've firmly incorporated the 5 C's in your skill-set and daily activities, you can help others do the same. Help them assess their strengths, desires, and needs, and help them create a development plan that not only supports the vision, mission, and goals of the organization, but also supports them in growing their career.

During the growth process we need to help others avoid beating themselves up when they encounter obstacles or failures. Rather, think in terms of what COULD be done to better oneself or the outcome. Ask and answer: "What have we learned and what changes COULD we make?

Are you ready to FLY? Are you equipped to help others lead themselves?

Tip 15

Knowing Your Team

*Great things in business are never
done by one person. They're done by
a team of people.* – Steve Jobs

Effective leadership sets the tone for entire teams and organizations, with team members provided a sense of inclusiveness, resulting in higher performance and goal attainment.

Patrick Lencioni (author of The Five Dysfunctions Of A Team) shares that successful teams utilize behaviors and skills with a focus on TRUST, COMMITMENT, ACCOUNTABILITY, RESULTS, and healthy CONFLICT.

So what can you as a leader do? Get started by knowing your team. Ask each team member:

- How do they like to be communicated to?

- Do they want daily interactions or only "as needed"?
- What do they like best about their job?
- Do they have career aspirations?
- Would they say the team trusts one another?
- Are they committed to supporting the team or do they prefer going "solo"?
- Do they hold themselves accountable and are they comfortable holding others accountable?
- Do they have the skills to respectfully discuss differences?
- What skill / behavior would they most want to develop?
- What do **you** do that they like best?
- Is there anything **you** do that they would like you to stop doing?

Have you held these conversations? What have you done to let your team know that you hear what they say, and that you're willing to take action to address their needs and suggestions?

Don't be the leader that devotes too much time to tasks and not enough time on your team. Relationships matter. If your team feels you genuinely care about them, they are likely to help you (and the organization) achieve more.

We found these acronyms to remind us of why teams matter:

TEAM   Time, Energy, And Money
TEAM   Together Everyone Accomplishes More

What are you doing to let your team know you're listening?

Tip 16

Good Boss /Bad Boss

A boss creates fear, a leader confidence. A boss fixes blame, a leader corrects mistakes. A boss knows all, a leader asks questions. A boss makes work drudgery, a leader makes it interesting.—Russell H. Ewing

Did you know that research shows that 17 percent of workers report being mistreated by their bosses? Gary Namie, author of "The Bully at Work" and a psychology professor says the victims are not only the employees but also the organizations they work for.

Bad bosses influence attrition, absenteeism, employee satisfaction and productivity levels, and quality overall. And, the most talented employees may cause a threat to incompetent bosses so ultimately they are the targets, are driven out of the organization, with the talent pool and bench strength of the organization impacted.

Here are some examples of actual "BAD BOSS" experiences:

- Crying while giving a performance evaluation
- Changing directions and approach every time another person became involved
- Taking credit for work done by others
- Unwilling to take risks
- Needs approval before making a decision
- Embarrasses others in front of colleagues
- Leads by intimidation

From an opposing perspective, "GOOD BOSS" experiences have included:

- Giving feedback in a meaningful, non hurtful way
- Recognizing and rewarding key contributions
- Addressing toxic behaviors
- Understands you can't be "everything to everyone"
- Providing development opportunities
- Becoming a mentor
- Views errors as learning experiences

Have you observed any of these behaviors? Any you want to avoid? What about to incorporate?

NOTE: National Boss Day (or Bosses Day) falls on October 16. Remember to recognize those that have positively influenced you!

Tip 17

Sources Of Pain

*For good ideas and true innovation,
you need human interaction, conflict,
argument, debate.*—Margaret Heffernan

Sources of pain. We're talking about at work. Do you know people that complicate your ability to deliver and achieve goals? Do they deflate the energy of those they work with? Perhaps they are:

- Disruptive
- Antagonistic
- Over committers
- Under performers
- Not reliable
- Lacking accountability
- Finger pointers
- Not accepting of differences or change
- Exhibits dictatorial behaviors

Some refer to these difficult individuals as sources of pain, and the situation/behavior that creates the difficulty must be managed (and the sooner the better).

Here are a few tips that can help:

- Evaluate whether you could have misunderstood the behavior
- Try to understand the intention behind the action
- Be respectful and factual – share your perception with the "source of pain" using facts
- Assess whether you are the only one experiencing the issue
- Don't focus only on the negative; could it just be a bad day or is it a consistent problem?
- Don't wait; address it immediately

Human interactions often include conflict, (simply a difference of opinion/perspective) and this can be inspiring, energizing, and thought provoking.

Just remember that it's up to us as leaders to address any actions/behaviors that negatively impact our ability to obtain desired results.

Tip 18

T.I.A – Trust, Integrity, Authenticity

*Honesty: Be true to others in all that
you do. Integrity; Be true to yourself in
all that you do.*—Dmitriy Kozlov

Trust, Integrity and Authenticity (T.I.A.). It's what makes teams thrive, earns leaders respect, and inspires team members to succeed.

It also builds individual and team confidence levels, and provides a sense of empowerment along with the willingness for innovative thinking and risk-taking.

A true leader builds a culture where accountability and responsibility are the "norm". There's no fear of bad reviews, demotions, or embarrassment.

TIPS:

- Assess whether there are any reasons others may not trust you. Work on them!
- Do you consistently display the behaviors you wish to see in others?
- How is your current work culture? What changes could be made to make it stronger?
- Select a highly trusted leader; identify the behaviors you feel make then successful and add them to your "tool-belt".
- ASK your team for their ideas about improving the culture; listen and be responsive!

Tip 19

Unpopular Decisions

*There are many qualities that make
a great leader. But having strong
beliefs, being able to stick with them
through popular and unpopular times,
is the most important characteristic of
a great leader.*—Rudy Giuliani

Being a leader includes making tough and unpopular decisions. It's not too hard when things are going well and when results and performance levels are in line with our goals.

As leaders, we won't always be popular, and with almost certainty we will have to make unpopular decision that don't feel good, but must be made to obtain desired results and grow our business (or even keep our company afloat).

Leadership requires courage, and yes, making unpopular decisions is part of it.

Here are some tips for communicating any decision:

- State why the decision needed to be made
- Indicate who will be impacted because of the
- decision
- Anticipate and prepare for questions and
- opposition
- Openly discuss both positive and negative impacts
- Listen and feel
- PRACTICE WHAT YOU'RE GOING TO SAY!

Changes, whether popular or unpopular need to be communicated. Think about what channel of communication you will use. Face to face is best, but not always possible. What would be most effective, from both the perspective of the message sender, and the receiver?

Leadership needs to be open and authentic, and there is a need to build trust across organizations. This is especially true during times of uncertainty and when unpopular decisions must be made. Leaders are expected to lead – to set the strategy and establish shared goals, and provide clarity about expectations ex. The who and the what

Which tips will help you communicate unpopular decisions?

Tip 20

A Happy Workplace

Even if you're not a business leader,
you can still take an active part
in a cultural transformation.—
FORTUNE March 2018

Would you say that you are part of a "happy workplace"? If yes, what's your rationale, and if no, what are the dis-satisfiers?

Company GREAT PLACE TO WORK summarized survey results for identifying the "100 Best Companies To Work For/2018". Millions of employees in more than 50 countries were surveyed to obtain perspectives about what makes an exemplary workplace.

The six components within the survey included: Values, Innovation, Financial Growth, Leadership Effectiveness, Maximizing Human Potential, and Trust.

Bottom line, it's all about how the workplace culture creates growth and excellence, and company **SalesForce** scored first place. The primary reason? **The corporate culture.** Note: Having a favorable work culture was the most common factor in the "100 Best Companies" list.

Some other commonalities included:

- Create a culture that can withstand conflict and varying views (even encourage it!)
- Create a culture of transparency
- Create a culture that is "open, friendly, diverse, and team oriented"
- Support your employees (at work and in their personal life)
- Ensure work/life balance is more than just a motto
- Remain neutral politically (regardless of your feelings)
- Invest in your people
- Truly embrace diversity
- Build trusting relationships between employees and management
- "Every voice matters" – engage employees of all levels
- Thank, appreciate, and reward successes
- Have clearly defined and unifying goals
- Offer flexible work hours
- Possess a desire to see others succeed
- Ensure your leadership team is caring, approachable, and inspiring

One final point, trust and inclusiveness are "must haves".

Tip 21

Adaptive and Agile

*Key components of being adaptive and agile
include placing an emphasis on teamwork
and continuous improvement, and of
course possessing a strong sense of values.
Make sure you incorporate the following
values within your team: focus, courage,
openness, commitment, and respect.*

During the last several years there has been a large push
towards faster delivery and a more rapid deployment
of solutions promoting innovation and growth. This is
wonderful news for using a creative energetic process that
permits out of the box thinking while increasing customer
satisfaction.

It no longer takes years for implementations to occur (or
for enhancements to be applied), but it does require a new

mindset, new processes, new tools, and of course skilled resources.

Our resources are the crux of the matter. We must continue to understand how people work, think, act and react, and we need to understand that the basic foundation of any team is trust. The faster you build it, the better it is for obtaining results!

Too often as technocrats we think that we can circumvent the people development side of the equation, and forget (or choose not to concern ourselves) about how we "show up", and limit our focus to the task at hand.

Get to know your team members! Understand one another, know the gifts or "Magic Dust™" of each team member, and honor, support, and leverage them. A strong sense of self awareness, and an awareness of what others are passionate about will inspire and release more occurrences of innovation and growth that will transcend your current business state.

Trust within teams fosters collaboration. Obstacles will be addressed and removed; and if the issue is out of their "scope" of responsibility, they will work with other teams that do have the authority to take action.

Communication is always key. Everyone must have, and must share information, so that decision making is effective, that problems and concerns are openly discussed, and that solutions are timely (immediate).

Be adaptive and agile and let your courage allow you to undertake greater challenges!

Tip 22

Clear As Mud

Without focusing and getting to clarity, you cannot lead. You cannot motivate. You cannot plan. You cannot communicate.—Bobb Biehl

Would you say you have clarity in your life, both personally and professionally, or would you lean more towards the "clear as mud" descriptor? Where are you in your career and where would you like to be? What about outside of work? Are you fulfilling your dreams?

Strategist/consultant Paul Cummings suggests thinking in terms of a camera:

- Most cameras today automatically know how to focus on an image.
- Years back that was not the case. You had to take the time (and make an effort) to focus your camera on the image you wanted to capture.

- You had to slowly twist and adjust the lens until the image looked clear and in focus.

He then goes on to share how our minds work:

- Minds don't come with an "autofocus" button
- Mental clarity is not simple
- It takes time and effort to find our clarity
- As leaders, we must take the time we need to find our own clarity, especially if we want to lead others. (Remember FLY? First Lead Yourself, then Lead Others)

Mental clarity means that you have total sharpness and clearness of mind about where you are and where you're headed.

That you have a clear perception and understanding of who you are and what you want to get out of life. If you want to lead others well, you must have total clarity about the things that you are wanting to accomplish. Examples: Goals? Expectations?

Team members are looking to their leader for confidence, total clarity and certainty. When clarity exists, you will be a trusted leader, and your team will want to follow you.

Some define CLARITY as knowing exactly what you want to achieve, and FOCUS as knowing which daily actions to take to get there.

Are you "Clear as Mud" or "Auto-Focused"?

Tip 23

Succession Planning

*Succession planning is a process for
identifying and developing internal people
with the potential to fill key leadership
positions within the organization.*

You lead a very successful team, your abilities have been recognized, and as a result have been offered a promotion.

Is your team ready for you to move on? Will there be an impact to the organization because of your move? Could your promotion be delayed because of not having a successor?

The big question is: What have YOU done to develop, mentor, and groom possible replacements?

Some companies have formal processes in place to fill leadership roles, others have informal processes, and some have nothing in place at all. As leaders, we want to ensure that our key roles, if vacated, will not present issues.

SUCCESSION PLANNING SUGGESTIONS:

- Create mentorships
- Utilize cross training
- Delegate leadership tasks
- Commit to leadership development
- Create and re-visit development plans
- Implement job shadowing
- Conduct talent reviews
- Identify high performers in your department
- Request a list of high performers across the organization
- Assess readiness levels and timeframes ex. now, in 1 year, in 2 years, etc
- Ensure the high performers WANT a leadership position! We once knew a person that was targeted for several promotional opportunities but had no desire to change roles!

Most employees WANT to be developed, and organizations have the need to build bench-strength; having a plan in place sounds like a win-win situation!

Tip 24

Activity Does NOT = Achievement

Never Mistake Activity for Achievement—JohnWooden

There are mixed opinions about whether effort should be rewarded in addition to results.

We too have varying thoughts. There are goals and initiatives that need to be attained by individuals, teams, and entire organizations. (That's how we survive and thrive).

As a leader, how do you feel when you see colleagues/direct reports committed to doing everything they can to achieve results, but are unsuccessful? Do you acknowledge their contributions even when success is not achieved?

Below are excerpts from Craig Impelman's perspectives published in SUCCESS magazine, based on John Wooden's achievement model:

1. Proper Execution of the Plan

A daily practice plan should be prepared and followed. If you fail to follow the program on one thing, it may affect others. If you planned poorly, make the corrections for the following day . . .

2. Attention to Detail

The coach should be on the floor early to make certain that everything is ready for practice. I like to have a checklist for the managers to go by, but the coach must make sure. Anticipate from past experience and be prepared.

3. Maximize use of time.

Even though a particular drill may be emphasizing one specific fundamental, other fundamentals in use should not be overlooked.

4. Post-Practice Analysis

I like to sit down with my assistants immediately after practice and briefly analyze and discuss the practice of that day.

These were written for basketball, so we'll put it in business terms:

- Create a plan (or goals) and identify all steps required (and possible roadblocks)
- As leaders, we don't need to execute the plan, but we need to clearly communicate the desired results and timeframes
- Remain focused and understand and incorporate dependencies and under-lying needs/skills
- Conduct a debrief after every initiative/deliverable. What worked well, what didn't, and what could you do differently next time to improve results?

Not everything is a success, nor does everything go as planned despite all of our efforts and critical contributions.

So, back to the original question "Do you acknowledge contributions even when success is not achieved?"

Tip 25

Got EQ?

*This world of ours... must avoid becoming
a community of dreadful fear and hate, and
be, instead, a proud confederation of mutual
trust and respect.*—Dwight D. Eisenhower

Do you think leaders must be emotionally intelligent? What about being aware of their impact on others? About how their words and delivery may be interpreted? And, what is our responsibility to expose poor leadership?

Can you imagine a leader in corporate America calling any person a "bimbo" or an "idiot"? How would the staff feel? What would peers think? Would it promote a team atmosphere? Would it play well with any partner, vendor partner, or customer? How would the stockholders feel? What could possibly be in a person's mind to degrade another person? What and why would a person continue to subject people to slanderous rants and raves and then be congratulated because they speak their mind?

If that is viewed as leadership, and strong leadership at that, we don't want any part of it. We doubt that there is a company on the planet that would tolerate name calling, or allow this kind of behavior to be proudly tweeted around the globe. If it's acceptable for one person to act that way, doesn't it give permission for others to act the same way? Regardless of your title, wealth, and known successes, this behavior is unacceptable. Period.

Our thoughts are that a leadership "must" is to give respect and dignity to everyone. Not because they've earned it but because they are people. If someone hurts your feelings is there a better way to handle the situation other than throwing around negative terms like "bimbo" and "idiot"? Is this the type of behavior we want to see in our children, our peers, and in society?

Can you imagine what our environment would be like if our bosses called us (or others), dumb, not smart, or slow? How would we feel? We've already seen various people downplay this behavior yet they likely would not tolerate this from a co-worker, a friend, or a family member.

All the work that has been done with leadership development can be thrown out the window if we are to view this kind of behavior as acceptable. We think it needs to be talked about. If we don't, that implies consent/acceptance and that simply is not the case. We need to hold ourselves and others accountable, and speak up, or we are no better than the person who makes disrespectful statements.

We must give feedback in a healthy, honoring, and respectful manner, and it is up to each of us to treat every person on the planet with the dignity and respect they deserve. We strongly support being true to oneself and being authentic, but we must also be emotionally intelligent.

Tip 26

More About EQ

*Research shows convincingly that EQ is
more important than IQ in almost every
role and many times more important in
leadership roles.*—Dr. Stephen R. Covey

Some consider EQ to be the single biggest predictor of performance in the workplace and the strongest driver of leadership and personal excellence. By developing our EQ, we position ourselves to more successfully cope with organizational demands and pressures.

Psychologist Steven Stein and psychiatrist Howard Book state that strong leaders have both a high IQ (Intelligence Quotient) and a developed EQ (Emotional Intelligence Quotient). Intelligence will only go so far; leaders must also be aware of how they present themselves, how they respond to others, and how others perceive them.

Our IQ is considered to be non-dynamic and is an indicator of how we perform intellectual tasks. Our EQ on the other hand can increase through self development and consists of 4 areas: *Self awareness, self management, social awareness, and relationship management.*

- Self Awareness is critical when engaging in communication
- Self Management is key for managing emotions in difficult situations
- Social Awareness leverages awareness of others to perform at your peak
- Relationship Management manages relationships to increase job performance and integrates EQ professionally and personally

Self-awareness and self-management are about you – do you know your strengths and weaknesses; are you a continual learner?

Social Awareness and Relationship Management are about how you interact with others. Are you in tune with their styles? Do you bring out the best in others?

Emotional intelligence is the genuine ability to feel emotions, understand what you're feeling and why, understand how others are feeling, and respond appropriately. Having a high EQ builds relationships and fosters communication even in the most difficult of times.

Do you know your EQ? More importantly, are you developing your EQ?

Tip 27

Appreciating Diversity

*Our greatest strength as a human race is
our ability to acknowledge our differences,
our greatest weakness is our failure to
embrace them.*—Judith Henderson

When you hear the word "diversity", what comes to mind?
Per the Bing dictionary, it can mean a *"variety of something
such as opinion, color, or style"*, it can be *"ethnic variety, as well
as socioeconomic and gender variety, in a group, society, or
institution"*, and it can be *"a discrepancy, or a difference from
what is normal or expected"*.

- Appreciating and Leveraging Diversity In The
  Workplace Has Benefits
- Knowledge, acceptance, and awareness are factors
  for becoming more diverse.

How accepting are you of differences? Would you consider yourself and your organization to be diverse? Do you appreciate differences, and do you leverage those differences to increase effectiveness?

Before you answer, think about what comes to mind when topics related to diversity and differences surface. Do you think about **race, culture, age, gender, sexual orientation and disabilities?**

Do you also think about **accents, education, physical size, spiritual orientation, and political preferences**?

Differences are limitless. What's key is our awareness, respect, and appreciation for how these differences strengthen our team, our organization, and our world.

We all have biases and filters. What we suggest is taking the time to examine our biases and recognize the impacts differences have on attitudes and actions with the ultimate goal to appreciate and utilize what's different.

Studies show that diversity enhances learning; we grow our mindset when we listen, process, and understand differences (and maybe learn that our way isn't the only way!)

Have you observed a variety of leadership skills, traits and behaviors within your organization? Do you relate equally to all styles? Do you find all of them effective? Chances are "no".

Be cognizant of how these differing styles make you feel and give thought as to why. Appreciating and valuing differences lends itself to having a stronger team and organization.

Tip 28

The Blame Game

*Concern yourself more with accepting
responsibility than with assigning blame.
Let the possibilities inspire you more than the
obstacles discourage you.*—Ralph Marston

We all make mistakes; what's key is how we handle/address them. Chances are when you experience negative feelings your energy level drops. This is normal. Looking for someone to blame, sadly, is also normal for some individuals and teams.

When errors occur, frustration levels grow, excuses get made, and finger pointing can sometimes run rampant. Surely there must be someone to blame!

Finding external causes initially makes one feel better; in actuality instead of being helpful, these behaviors accomplish little, they waste energy, and they cause ill feelings.

Healthier approaches include:

- Accept responsibility (assigning blame creates obstacles to success).
- Drill down on the reason for the error, seek solutions, and consider alternative approaches. What could have been done differently to prevent the problem? What can be done so there is not a reoccurrence? Do processes need to change? Were the right resources involved?
- Avoid asking "why" as it places blame and puts people and teams on the defensive.
- Replace the word "should" with the word "could". (It provides options, and there isn't necessarily only one correct choice). Ex. What COULD we have done differently?
- Do get to the root cause, identify and remove roadblocks, remove emotion and remain fact based.
- Look at replacing unfavorable behaviors with those having a positive influence.
- If you've erred, own it, learn from it and move on. You can't "undo" it, but you can take measures to prevent a reoccurrence.

We're responsible for our actions and behaviors and how we choose to modify them. We can influence others, but it's their choice as to whether they're willing to change.

Placing blame reduces the power to change and grow; don't play the blame game!

Tip 29

Feedback's For Champions

*Feedback is the breakfast of
champions.*—Ken Blanchard

Throughout the course of each year, there are a few things we
must consistently do. We need to take a check-point on the
status of our goals, we need to assess development planning
actions, and we need to consistently provide feedback, as
well as request feedback.

How are you at providing feedback to your staff or team
members? Has your leader provided you with feedback?
Assuming yes, was the feedback constructive and helpful?

If you have direct reports, we recommend you commit to
providing formal feedback on a monthly basis. This can
include the status of goals, (what's on track versus any
misses), the execution of roles and responsibilities, and any
new priorities.

In addition, there's a need to provide immediate feedback such as recognition for a job well done, going above and beyond, unproductive behaviors, development needs, etc). A critical reminder: ***feedback must be well intended, delivered with respect, and in an honoring manner.***

As leaders, we may be more comfortable giving feedback than receiving it. We all have perceptions as to how our co-workers, direct reports, business partners and customers would evaluate us, but few of us actually solicit feedback on a regular basis.

When's the last time you completed a formal feedback process?

We suggest utilizing a coach to help you understand the candid, honest and constructive feedback you'll receive. Determine what you're especially effective at, find out how you could be even more effective, obtain suggestions on how your behaviors could be enhanced, and update your development plan accordingly.

Feedback and self-improvement take time, courage, ambition, and the desire to change. Are you game?

Tip 30

Mentor Power

*Mentor: Someone whose hindsight can
become your foresight.*—unknown

How do you define the role of mentor? We define it as
*"someone who imparts wisdom and shares knowledge with a less
experienced person"*.

Mentors share their experiences (both negative and positive/
what went well and what did not, and WHY), and they help
pave the way for their mentee to attain desired goals and
career aspirations.

Part of the mentor's role is to:

- Provide meaningful, consistent, and timely feedback
- Explore strengths and developmental needs
  (technical and interpersonal)

- Discuss networks that will help grow career relationships and opportunities
- Ensure trust and integrity exist for all interactions
- Have ongoing and open communication
- Set realistic expectations

Mentoring may be formal or informal, but the expectations and roles should be defined and agreed to at the inception of the relationship.

- What's the purpose of the mentorship?
- What type of expertise/guidance is the mentee seeking?
- How often will you meet?

Note: In general, mentors/mentees do not have a reporting relationship which allows for more candid discussions.

As a leader, are you open to assisting others with achieving their career aspirations? Are you willing to share your wisdom and experiences with others to help them grow? If yes, you have MENTOR POWER!

__Tip 31__

What Keeps You Up?

*The quality of a leader is reflected in the
standards they set for themselves.*—Ray Kroc

It's a given that leadership will have its challenges. What's
important is to understand what we're doing about them. We
need to assess what **aren't** we doing that we could, and what
are we doing that may not be serving us well.

A leadership survey was conducted that asked how prepared
the leaders were in the following 4 areas:

1. Innovation
2. Human Capital
3. Operational Excellence
4. Customer Relationships

The results found:

Customer Relationships scored highest with 45% of leaders feeling they were well prepared.

This was followed with Operational Excellence at 33%. (Wikipedia defines this as "an element of organizational leadership that stresses the application of a variety of principles, systems, and tools toward the sustainable improvement of key performance metrics").

Innovation (26%) and Human Capital (27%) were areas where leaders felt a little less prepared. (Human capital, as defined by Wikipedia is the stock of knowledge, habits, social and personality attributes, including creativity, embodied in the ability to perform labor so as to produce economic value).

Does it surprise you that the highest score is 45%? That for three of the four challenges, less than one third of the leaders surveyed felt they were well prepared to address the challenge?

Skill-set and experience might come to mind for the low scores, but it turns out the top obstacles for growth included:

- Not enough time or opportunity
- Lack of support/autonomy
- Lack of skill or knowledge

Leaders also shared that they wanted more engagement from Human Resources, Senior Management, Managers, and the employees themselves.

The people factor seems to be the top "want and need". Collaboration, focus, mentorships, ownership, accountability, and time all seem to play a role.

Having clear priorities and shared goals are also an absolute must have. Experiencing change and facing challenges are inevitable, so leaders (remember we're all leaders!), must continually develop their skills to manage internal and external challenges they are facing.

What's keeping you up? What could help?

Tip 32

Respect and Leadership

Respect is the key determinant of high-performance leadership. How much people respect you determines how well they perform.—Brian Tracey

Would you consider yourself to be a respectful person and a respectful leader? Do you consider your co-workers, customers, and business partners respectful? There are arguments that levels of respect are diminishing; that we care less about others, and that we may even care less about ourselves.

Let's define RESPECT. Wikipedia says: *Respect denotes a positive feeling of esteem . . . and it can be a specific feeling of regard for the actual qualities of the one respected (e.g., "I have great respect for her judgment")*

It also says: *Respect should not be confused with tolerance, since tolerance doesn't necessarily imply any positive feeling, and is compatible with contempt, which is the opposite of respect.* Interesting distinction; respect MUST include positive feelings.

Some say respect must be earned; does this really serve us well? What if we begin all relationships on a basis of respect, where we look for desirable qualities and seek positive feelings? Let's at least start on a level playing field and give others the benefit of the doubt that they are indeed respectful with a need to be respected.

So what can we do as leaders to build respect and be respected?

- We need to be authentic, walk the talk, follow through with what we commit to, and support and reward the attainment of our goals.
- We need to take time to build relationships with everyone we interact with.
- We need to give (and receive) feedback in a constructive and honoring way.
- We need to address unproductive behaviors and hold others accountable.
- We need to expect that conflict will occur, and realize that it is healthy and promotes growth. (Remember, conflict is a difference of desires or opinions, where your concerns or the concerns of someone else are not shared).
- We need to respect and admire who we are and what we have achieved and ensure team members do the same.

Increasing levels of respect not only fosters success but also improves morale, decreases attrition, and enhances job satisfaction.

Tip 33

Leadership Killers

*The supreme quality for leadership is
unquestionably integrity. Without it, no real
success is possible, no matter whether it is on
a section gang, a football field, in an army,
or in an office.*—Dwight D. Eisenhower

We like to think that as leaders, we consistently strive to become more effective, take actions to develop our weaknesses, and commit to enhancing our skill-set.

Self-development requires awareness, a willingness to change, and it's rarely immediate or easy. It also requires accepting feedback, and listening to what is NOT working. Enter the **LEADERSHIP KILLERS:**

- Lack of integrity/trust
- Lack of walking the talk
- Over-promising/under-delivering

- Inaccuracies/un-substantiation
- Lack of accountability/passing the buck
- Over-optimism/over-pessimism
- Lack of support (not having their back)

Trust is at the top. As leaders, we must build strong relationships with our staff/team members as well as with others we regularly interact with. Make that #1 in your development plan!

We need to be known for saying what we mean, and modeling the behaviors and skills we expect from others.

We need to own up to our errors and failures, and help our team learn and grow from their mistakes.

We know it isn't easy, we know it requires courage and commitment, and we know we may need to step out of our comfort zone.

Do you know what is NOT working well for you or your team? Do any of the Leadership Killers need to be addressed?

Tip 34

A Multi Generational Workplace

*Managing multigenerational workforces is
an art in itself. Young workers want to make
a quick impact, the middle generation needs
to believe in the mission, and older employees
don't like ambivalence.*—Eric J. McNully

Does your workplace consist of a blend of multi generations?
Do the differences add synergy or perhaps increase conflict?
Let's break it down into 5 generations (as reported by Katrina
Plourde):

- **Silent Generation** – born during the Great
  Depression and WWII (1925-1942)
- **Baby Boomers** (1943-1964)
- **Generation X** (1965-1976)
- **Generation Y** (1977-1994)
- **Millennials** (1994 -)

The intent is not to label people, but rather share the perceptions of what each generation is known for.

The **Silent Generation** was considered hard working, optimistic, accountable, financially savvy, and optimistic about the future.

Baby Boomers are considered to have strong workplace and family ideals and traditions, are relatively active, and uncertain what the future may hold.

Gen X folks are thought to live in the present, like to experiment, desire immediate results, and may question authority. They also may be selfish and cynical.

Gen Y / Millenials. Some consider these one and the same. Both are considered materialistic, selfish, and maybe even disrespectful. They are aware of the world, are technologically savvy, and may feel a sense of entitlement with high workplace expectations.

It's not all flattering, and we know these are generalizations, but the work culture may be impacted. As leaders, do you view this as an opportunity so the strengths of each generation can be leveraged, or do you view it as a thorn, and not quite certain what (if anything) you need to do?

Consider if your team is truly a team or if it consists of a group of individuals with their own agenda. Do they have shared goals and do they work together to achieve them? Do they willingly share their skills and listen for the value others bring to the team? Can they be candid with one another and discus differences/conflict in a healthy manner?

Bottom line, what are you doing to create synergy within your multi generational workplace?

Tip 35

Divisive Or Inclusive?

The effect of leadership failure on any
organization of people is the same:
Polarization, instability, and if left
unchecked, destruction.—Steve Tobak

We enjoy providing tips and sharing stories about becoming a more effective leader, and we also like to discuss optimal behaviors and skill-sets that the strongest leaders possess. Why? Because if we don't continually work at being our best, we may find that we have unintentionally created instability or uncertainty, and find that our team is floundering.

Effective leaders set the tone for their entire team/ organization. They share their vision, mission, goals, and strategies, and they create and communicate a roadmap for reaching the desired point of destination.

They focus on inclusiveness. They communicate. They clarify how each colleague can contribute to achieving shared goals. They help everyone understand how and why they each have a role, helping minimize obstacles within the roadmap.

In Deloitte Insights, Juliet Bourke and Bernadette Dillon published The Six Signature Traits Of Inclusive Leadership:

1. COGNIZANCE - Bias is a leaders Achilles heel
2. CURIOSITY - Different ideas and experiences enable growth
3. CULTURAL INTELLIGENCE – Not everyone sees the world through the same cultural frame
4. COLLABORATION - A diverse thinking team is greater than the sum of its parts
5. COMMITMENT – Staying the course is hard
6. COURAGE – Talking about imperfections involves personal risk taking

We agree, and equate them to PeopleTek's terminology:

- **Awareness** - of self and others and the value provided
- **Continual learning** – never get complacent or lose the desire to improve and listen to differing perspectives
- **Emotional Intelligence**- understand the difference between IQ and EQ and leverage the strengths
- **Collaboration** – working together to find a solution is a win-win

- **Accountability**, persistence and commitment – don't give up despite barriers or failures
- **Courage** - We coined the term CourageAbility™ (and wrote a book about it – 12 Steps For Courageous Leadership)

The concepts are pretty similar; what's key is that we incorporate them into our behaviors, modeling them for others to reflect on, and hopefully emulate.

Tip 36

Stressed?

Stress is an important dragon to slay – or at least tame – in your life.—Marilu Henner

How's your stress level at work? Would you say it's occasional or fairly consistent?

The first step in handling stress is to be aware of it. Without awareness, stress is in control of you and not the other way around.

Do a simple assessment of the components below, rating your stress level for each as "Low", "Medium", or "High".

Job role/characteristics

Too demanding
Not what I thought it was going to be

Work Benefits/compensation

Difficult to get a promotion
Low compensation

Work Schedule

No flexibility
Creates conflict

Work Relationships

None
Conflict ridden

Boss Relationship

Not valued/skills not utilized
Minimal direction / recognition

How many did you rate "high"? We suggest addressing those first. Balance is the key to managing stress; consider what you can do differently to lower your stress levels.

Are you trying too hard? We often have a self-imposed need to compete that adds to our stress. We also don't take time for the 3 R's: Re-charge, re-energize, and relax!

Build in time each day for things you enjoy. (Music, exercise, reading, family time). While at work, stand, stretch, take a walk, and don't procrastinate. Putting off tasks will only add to your stress.

Tip 37

Boss Versus Leader

The best bosses aren't bosses – they are leaders.—Stephanie Sarkis, Ph.D.

One of our clients, Praveen Challa, provided us with the following differentiators:

A Boss . . .	**A Leader . . .**
Drives employees	Coaches employees
Depends on authority	Depends on goodwill
Inspires fear	Generates enthusiasm
Says "I"	Says "We"
Places blame for breakdowns	Fixes the breakdown
Knows how it's done	Shows how it's done
Uses people	Develops people
Takes credit	Gives credit
Commands	Asks

A Boss . . .

Says "go"

A Leader . . .

Says "let's go"

In our interactions with individuals and teams, we've had the following thoughts shared about what a great leader is. Some include:

Great leaders are great listeners. They listen closely and make others feel that they've been heard.

Great leaders genuinely care about their staff's careers and not just about performing tasks. They conduct one-on-one sessions with their staff and provide mentoring and coaching, and review each individual's progress against development plans.

Great leaders understand and appreciate differences and respond to individuals in their preferred style. They accept that everyone is unique and special, and adapt their styles as needed, ultimately strengthening relationships and improving results.

Great leaders stretch their people to excellence and provide meaningful feedback.

Great leaders are "in the boat" with you and have compassion for the things you're experiencing. You can feel their involvement; they make themselves visible and available during difficult times.

Great leaders truly feel PEOPLE come first, and their actions and behaviors reflect this. They're authentic, mean what they say, and deliver on what was committed to.

Are there any behaviors you could change to become a stronger leader?

Tip 38

Managing "UP"

Managing "UP" requires that you manage to the expectations of your boss: Know their priorities. Speak their language. Anticipate their needs. Be truthful and don't BS them. Contract properly at the end of a meeting.—Achim Nowak

How do you feel about the leadership skills you possess? Would you rate yourself "average", "above average", or maybe even "below average"?

When you rated yourself, which skills did you consider? Did you limit it to those that impact the interactions and relationships with your direct reports and perhaps your peers? What we often forget to include is the critical relationship required with our boss.

Here are some reminders:

- Learn your boss' communication style. - What level of detail do they prefer?
- Be proactive – share strengths and ideas and create an executable plan.
- Meet regularly - discuss progress against goals and areas for improvement.
- Ask for your boss' opinion - Ask for their perspective on things.
- Go to your boss with solutions – ask for help when needed, but do your "homework"
- Develop a power that makes you attractive - stay apprised of changes in your industry, understand your competitors, have a strong customer/business partner relationship, be indispensible
- Address problems – talk about your differences; remain fact based; keep your emotions in check.
- Play devil's advocate – share your different perspective; say "Let me play devil's advocate" and add new perspectives.

Also, let your boss know that you appreciate him/her. Be authentic; provide genuine feedback. It's rare that bosses are told "well done"!

In order to "Manage UP", it's up to us to build a strong relationship with our boss. We need to ensure our expectations are aligned, that we have a clear understanding of our organization's vision, mission, and goals, that all of our behaviors support them, and that we are committed to making a difference.

Tip 39

What's My Message?

The art of communication is the language of leadership.—James Humes

We think we're good communicators, we think our message is understood; we're often wrong.

Levels of understanding differ and it's up to us as leaders to assess each situation. We need to adapt to differing styles and we need to remember that communication is not a one way exchange. Most importantly, we need to remember to communicate with others in THEIR language.

- What level of detail is desired?
- Should the "bottom line" message come first with supporting details to follow?
- Avoid getting too "wordy"
- Ensure your message is organized and your grammar correct; plan and prepare!

- Don't race through your message; be aware of the speed in which you're speaking
- If it's a complex message, break it down into smaller bullet points
- Allow time for your message to be processed
- If there will be impacts, share what they will be
- Are there any takeaways or expectations? Request they be repeated back

Everyone has a story about communication gone wrong – the delivery was well intended but somehow the message was garbled. (This happens both professionally and personally).

If you are the sender, ask the receiver to share what they heard, and ask for their perceptions. If you're the receiver, and especially when the message seems off, ask for clarity.

Perceptions left un-discussed can haunt us.

Tip 40

Self Control

Self-control is an essential quality for any leader and team if they are going to perform near to their capability. It is necessary that the leader demonstrates self-control if he expects his team to have self-control.—Craig Impelman

How's your self-control? When your "buttons" are being pushed can you immediately feel the discomfort? And, despite this ill feeling, do you have the ability to think calmly and respond appropriately? It's not easy.

Having the skill to respond with purpose and remain composed is something that we as leaders need to strive for on a daily basis. We need to continually improve our communication, interactions and relationships with our staff, customers, and situations.

Our level of effectiveness is directly tied to self-control and being aware. We all have hot buttons and we all know individuals that seem to have a "gift" to light those buttons up. Some common items that lend themselves to control issues include:

- Inaccurate/incomplete information
- Not being informed of problems
- Insubordination
- Lack of commitment or accountability
- Lack of effort and collaboration

When things happen that we didn't expect, others are watching us to see how we respond. Once we lose our composure, the damage is done and may not be recovered from even when our composure is restored.

Highly effective leaders are in control of their emotions at all times. We may need to postpone a response, use the restroom, or take an "urgent" call allowing us time to regroup and regain our control.

Remaining calm under pressure takes work; don't avoid those "urgent calls" when needed.

Tip 41

The Real Deal

*Authenticity is the alignment of head, mouth,
heart, and feet - thinking, saying, feeling,
and doing the same thing - consistently.
This builds trust, and followers love
leaders they can trust.*—Lance Secretan

We've already talked about authentic leadership; how it impacts the workplace, relationships, performance and profits.

When you hear "authentic leadership", what does that mean to you? Some describe it as:

- Being self-aware
- Being transparent
- Being true to yourself and others
- Sharing your strengths
- Understanding and developing your weaknesses
- The "Real Deal"

Wikipedia says the following:

Authentic leadership is an approach to leadership that emphasizes building the leader's legitimacy through honest relationships with followers which value their input and are built on an ethical foundation.

The words that stand out for us are LEGITIMACY, HONEST, VALUE and ETHICAL. Do a quick self-assessment and score yourself on the importance of those words, and how they align with your behaviors.

How did you self assess: LEGITIMACY, HONEST, VALUE and ETHICAL? Did anything stand out? Now assess your boss – how'd they do?

Other things to reflect on include:

- What's the purpose of my leadership?
- Does my current profession utilize my talents?
- Do I ever check my beliefs at the office door?
- How often do I feel pressured to compromise my values?
- Can I develop close relationships with my subordinates and still achieve my objectives?

To be truly authentic, validate what's important to you and align your personal and professional lives accordingly.

As a leader, help others do the same and become known as the "Real Deal"!

Tip 42

Critical C's For Self Awareness

The key to an ideal workplace, in one hyphenated word, is this: self-awareness.—Neil Blumenthal

In tip #14 (First Lead Yourself), we talked about the need for the 5 C's to be part of a leaders skill-set. Since our awareness levels are hopefully growing, let's complete a self assessment and see how we're doing.

Rate yourself 1 - 10 in each category (10 = highly effective); any area that scores less than 8 can be considered a target growth area):

	SCORE
Clarity	_____
Communication	_____
Coaching	_____

Courage   _____

Compassion   _____

Per Zig Ziglar "*you must make a choice to take a chance or your life will never change*", so we're adding 3 more C's. Now rate:

SCORE

Choices   _____

Chances   _____

Changes   _____

Some may be easier to rate than others; ask colleagues, trusted friends, and even family members how they would rate you. It's a simple form of feedback that may provide you with some great insights. It's also a great starting point to identify where you are today, and gets you thinking about where you want to be.

Determine what's most important to you and listen to your inner voice. What behaviors can you modify? Eliminate? Incorporate?

We all benefit from increasing our awareness levels as it enhances relationships, improves results, and drives us to be a more effective leader. Where will you start?

Tip 43

Hire Hard

*Great vision without great people
is irrelevant.*—Jim Collins

Hire Hard. What does this mean? Simply put, you need to invest the time, energy, and perhaps money to ensure you hire the right person for the right job. If you don't, the result is that you will be "managing hard" (investing even more time and energy after the fact on a daily basis).

Hiring hard provides:

> *Increased employee performance and productivity; Increased employee engagement, and Increased employee retention.*-- Keith Tatley

Hiring that "right person" is a challenge faced by all leaders. It's important to be clear on job functions, responsibilities and behaviors to help grow results. It's also equally important to spend sufficient time looking for qualified candidates that would be a good fit for your organization.

Global Resource Partners state you first must have a clear understanding of:

- The skills and experience required for the position
- The culture
- Objectives
- Conditions

You must then assess the applicants:

- Talent
- Behaviors
- Motivation
- Circumstances

Are there linkages? Are the applicant's behaviors aligned with your work culture and do they support your objectives?

Your hiring options may include both external and internal candidates; both have benefits, both have disadvantages. High potential employees will already be familiar with the culture, and it saves hiring costs, but you may need someone "fresh".

As leaders, we need to understand the skills, talent, and passion the applicant will bring to our organization. It's also important to know it's easier it develop skills than it is to change behaviors.

Bottom line, "hire hard so you can manage easy".

Tip 44

Career Coaching

*Coaching Is The Universal Language
of Change and Learning.*—CNN

Why is Career Coaching gaining in popularity? Generally speaking, the value of coaching is now being realized. Twenty some years ago, companies most often utilized a coach to help manage/address toxic behaviors. That still exists, but more commonly today, coaching engagements occur so high-potential performers become high performers as well as more influential, inspiring, and impactful leaders.

Joy McGovern, Ph.D shares:

- Coaching translates into doing
- Doing translates into impacting the business
- This impact can be quantified and maximized

Coaches frequently help their client with leadership/ management skills and behaviors, and with enhancing communication styles. The coaching engagement includes having a clear purpose, exploring improvement opportunities, agreements for action, and a commitment for change.

The coach validates perceived strengths, and will likely discuss behaviors that may be under-used or over-used. They listen, they inquire without passing judgment, and they increase awareness levels.

The coach / client engagement also includes exploring possibilities. The coach provides guidance for moving forward, they are a sounding board, and they remind the client of their purpose and commitments.

The value and benefits of coaching have been reported as having tangible business impacts:

- Productivity
- Quality
- Organizational Strength
- Fewer customer complaints

And also intangible business impacts:

- Improved Relationships (with direct reports, senior leaders, peers, etc)
- Improved Teamwork

- Reduced Conflict
- Increased Organizational Commitment

A simple recap of how the bottom line is impacted:

Career Coaching and Career Development =
Organizational Bench-Strength and Greater Results

Tip 45

Are You An Avoider?

*The whole business starts with ideas, and
we're convinced that ideas come out of an
environment of supportive conflict, which
is synonymous with appropriate friction.*—
Michael Eisner, former Disney CEO

Many leaders struggle with addressing conflict – are you one
of them? Would you consider yourself an "avoider"?

We've already shared that as leaders, we need to understand
the different styles of conflict and their appropriate usage,
and we need to remember that conflict is simply any situation
where one's concerns or desires differ from those of another.

Having teams that engage in healthy conflict can promote
growth. Team members that feel they are in a "safe"
environment will not only build upon the ideas of others,

but will be comfortable presenting opposing views and share thoughts that can inspire and promote new ways of thinking.

Enter the Avoider. Avoiding the need to address conflict has its appropriate time and place, but most often, leaders that are "avoiders" are labeled as weak, unassertive and uncooperative. That's not always the case!

Avoiding is appropriate when:

- There's a need to obtain additional details / facts
- Emotions are high and those involved need to cool down in order to think rationally
- The conflict is being addressed in a healthy manner and an "intervention" is not required by you!
- The timing is "not right" (ex. location, attendees, sensitive nature)

Conflict in the workplace is unavoidable; what's key is to prevent the conflict from escalating into an unhealthy situation. Productivity, communication, collaboration, inspiration, morale, and growth will all suffer if not properly managed.

Your response to managing and addressing conflict is entirely up to you. We do however need to understand the styles of conflict and when to effectively use them.

And yes, being an "avoider" has a time and place!

Tip 46

Listen To Influence

Want to become a better leader? Stop talking and start listening.—Mike Myatt

Are you familiar with the LEAP model?

- Listen
- Empathize
- Agree
- Plan

Originally developed by Dr. Xavier Amador for dealing with medical issues, it's also a great tool in the business world.

As leaders we need the ability to influence others regardless of reporting structure. Leadership styles and behaviors have changed over the past couple of decades (thankfully!), and gone are the days of dictatorial styles.

We now understand that influence consists of building and maintaining relationships and focusing on interpersonal skills in order to effectively drive and obtain desired results.

Development Dimensions International, Inc has been conducting leadership studies for over 40 years and found that "only a slight majority (55 percent) of leaders feel that they and their peers are engaged in mutual influence".

They also reported that communication skills, especially those related to listening, have ranked as the #1 skill for impacting high performance. And more specifically, listening and responding with empathy obtains the best results.

Empathic listeners are active listeners. They don't judge and they respond to the speaker so they know they've been heard.

Listen to what others are thinking and feeling, listen to their ideas and perceived obstacles – all will position you to more effectively influence others.

Tip 47

Workaholism Is Problematic

*It's all about quality of life and finding
a happy balance between work and
friends and family.*—Philip Green

Workaholism has become such a problem that many are
calling it 'the addiction of this century.'

How would you describe your work/life balance? Would
you be surprised to learn that 10-25% of us are considered
workaholics?

Our pace is quicker than ever before, and the ease and
ability to stay connected can be a plus, but it can also be
detrimental. Few of us excel at saying "enough is enough",
and we rarely remind our colleagues or staff to ensure a
work/life balance exists.

The Faculty of Psychology from The University of Bergen and Nottingham Trent University in the UK created "The Bergen Work Addiction Scale". Rate the questions below on a scale of 1 (never) to 5 (always):

1. You think of how you can free up more time to work _____
2. You spend much more time working than initially intended _____
3. You work in order to reduce feelings of guilt, anxiety, helplessness or depression _____
4. You have been told by others to cut down on work without listening to them _____
5. You become stressed if you are prohibited from working _____
6. You de-prioritize hobbies, leisure activities, and/or exercise because of your work _____
7. You work so much that it has negatively influenced your health _____

If you scored 4 (often) or 5 (always) on four or more of the criteria, that classifies you as a workaholic. How'd you do? Is it time to re-assess your work/life balance and set boundaries? Here are some ideas:

- Pick 2 days a week when you will limit your work day to 8 hours
- Pick 2-3 days a week when you commit to not doing additional work at home
- And, assess (based on your role) how much time is truly needed to be available each evening, on weekends, and while on vacation or holiday.

Studies have concluded that people who work 50 or more hours per week were likely to experience both physical and emotional consequences.

So, while it may seem like a good idea to work those long hours and attempt to achieve more, we can actually reduce our productivity level, increase error rates, and impact relationships.

Make sure to build in leisure time for doing the things you enjoy, for spending sufficient time with family and friends, and for "refresh" time!

Tip 48

Poor Communication

The single biggest problem in communication is the illusion that it has taken place –George Bernard Shaw

Communication. This single word is the root of many of our leadership issues. We think we're being clear, we think our message has been understood, we think our colleagues are onboard and aligned with us, with our strategies, and with our intent. WRONG!

Studies report that the cost of poor or mis-communication has hit an overwhelming $37 billion, and that $26,041 is the cumulative cost per worker per year due to productivity losses resulting from communication barriers. Wow!

On the positive side, studies also report that leaders with effective communication skills produced a 47 percent higher return to shareholders over a five-year period. That's big.

We all have different styles and behaviors and as a result we process and interpret things differently. HRDQ shares that there are 4 basic communication styles; review the chart below and select the style you feel best describes you.

Direct:

Gets to the bottom line, Speaks forcefully, Maintains eye contact, Presents position strongly

Spirited:

Persuasive, is a good story-teller, Focuses on the big picture, Uses motivational speech

Considerate:

Listens well, Is a good counselor, Uses supportive language, Builds trust

Systematic:

Presents precisely, Focus on facts, Efficient on speech, Well organized workplace

Based on style differences it's easy to understand how messages get muddled. Consider how the systematic communicator who focuses on facts might have clarity issues with those having the spirited style where the primary focus is on the big picture?

Don't assume your message was accurately interpreted; ask for a recap of what was "heard" and align expectations and any next steps.

Tip 49

Team Roles

The way a team plays as a whole determines its success. You may have the greatest bunch of individual stars in the world, but if they don't play together, the club won't be worth a dime.—Babe Ruth

Whether you lead a team, or are a team member, what's your vision for a successful team? Are you looking for any particular skill-set, behaviors, or traits?

Most of us would agree that the team needs a common purpose with a desire to achieve shared goals. We've learned from Patrick Lencioni that having trust in one another is the foundation for team success, and that team members must hold themselves and team members accountable.

What else do you look for in team members?

Allen Fahden and Srinvasan Namakkal conducted team studies for decades and determined that there are four critical team roles required for success. They are:

CREATOR: Generates the concepts and ideas; looks for solutions that may be unusual or unique; goes beyond the obvious. Creators generate fresh, creative and original ideas, recognizes alternatives and sees the "big picture". Once the idea is generated it gets passed to an Advancer.

ADVANCER: Recognizes ideas and new directions early on and develops ways to promote them. Advancers plan based on past experiences and successful methods, prefer familiar ideas and but are open to new concepts and will not be discouraged by rules and boundaries. Once there is structure toward implementation the idea is passed to a Refiner.

REFINER: Concepts are challenged and a methodical process is used to analyze, apply order, and look for flaws or possible problems with the concept or idea. Refiners are good at reviewing ideas and implementation plans, at modifying and coming up with new ideas, and rationally reviewing them to ensure success. The final pass of is to the Executor. If the concept or idea is not ready for implementation, the Advancer and Creator may get re-engaged, execute their role and then re-pass it to the Refiner.

EXECUTOR: Team objectives are followed up on and ideas and solutions are implemented. The Executor focuses on ensuring the implementation plan is orderly and has been well thought out and strives for high quality results.

They enjoy their tasks and the responsibility of final implementation but prefer that others take the lead.

One other role is critical to the success of a team; the **FLEXER**. The Flexer objectively monitors the contributions of the team members, keeps them moving in the right direction, and steps in as needed.

Teams benefit from having all roles filled as it gives them a competitive edge for promoting innovation and team synergy.

Do you have a well rounded team? Is there any role that dominates? Is there any role that needs filling?

Tip 50

Your Accountable Self

Accept responsibility for your life. Know that it is you who will get you where you want to go, no one else.—Les Brown

Do you consider accountability as one of your stronger traits?

Let's start by defining it:

The quality or state of being accountable; an obligation, willingness and commitment to accept responsibility or to account for one's actions.

It's strictly up to us - no one can make us be accountable. They may influence us, they may provide us with feedback, they may even put us on an improvement plan, but ultimately the choice is ours.

The first step is to clearly understand expectations

- What are the desired end results?
- How do we personally contribute to their achievement?
- Do we have any role in adding clarity or helping others understand their involvement?

The next step is to be honest with ourselves

- What are we committing to?
- Are the tasks and associated timeframes realistic?
- Do we have the required skill-set?
- Do we need others to guide or assist us?
- Are we able to admit mistakes when they occur?
- Do we openly communicate and engage others when we get off track?
- Are there other projects/priorities that may impact our commitments? Make them known!

Don't be afraid to say "no". Give thought to what you're agreeing to; if you feel your commitment could be at risk, be open about it. Saying "yes" may not always serve you well.

On a scale of 1-10, where would you rank yourself on accountability? Is there anything you could change?

Tip 51

Disengaged?

Coming together is a beginning.
Keeping together is progress. Working
together is success.—Henry Ford

Employee disengagement continues to be a workplace issue, but we're happy to share that there has been slight improvement over the past 5 years.

Workplace studies reflect that approximately:

- 31% of workers are engaged
- 51% are just showing up
- 18% are actively disengaged

Engaged employees are defined as those who are enthusiastic about their work, and committed to supporting shared vision, mission, goals, and strategies.

Improvement (albeit slight) is attributed to annual assessments being done in the workplace. Leaders are asking their staff / team for their opinions, and leadership is listening.

There are also 2 more things that DO make a difference:

1. Individual and team development is encouraged
2. Opportunities are provided allowing individuals to do what they do best (you've heard us speak about "magic dust™", which is each person's passion, special skill-set and strengths)

Engagement levels grow when:

- Individuals have a work / life balance
- Individual and team talent is utilized
- Passion, energy, and focus are leveraged
- Individuals/leaders learn to fulfill their own vision, and assist others to fulfill theirs
- Individuals/leaders are persistent and don't give up easily and encourage others to do the same

As an individual, what actions are you taking to increase your level of engagement?

As a leader, do you have a goal to increase engagement levels for your team?

Tip 52

One Thing

The quality of a person's life is in direct proportion to their commitment to excellence, regardless of their chosen field of endeavor.—Vince Lombardi

You've now read 51 tips to increase leadership effectiveness and improve results. If you had to pick just one thing you wanted to change in your behavior, what would it be?

It could be related to your professional life (for you as an individual, or for your team/organization), or it could be related to your personal life.

From an individual perspective:

- Where do you want to be more impactful? (personally or professionally)

- What areas would you like to see grow? (financially or intellectually)
- Are there relationships that need to be developed or enhanced?
- Does communication need to be addressed - is it insufficient or lacking clarity?
- Is there a commitment to continual learning?
- Does complacency have any role?
- How's the home / work balance?

From an organizational perspective, do colleagues:

- Trust one another?
- Engage in healthy conflict?
- Commit to decisions?
- Hold one another accountable?
- Focus on achieving collective results?
- Does the work culture support the agile mind-set?
- Is risk taking encouraged?
- Are differences such as values, culture, and diverse strengths recognized, appreciated, and valued?

Answer the following: (write them down!)

- What's **one** thing you want to change?

- Who's help do you need to make it become reality?

- Are there any barriers preventing your success?

Keep In Touch!

We'd love to hear from you.

- Which tips provided the greatest "a-ha" moment?

- Are there any tips you'd like to share with us?

- Visit our website and sign up for more weekly tips. www.peopletekcoaching.com

About the Authors

Michael W. Kublin created PeopleTek, a leadership coaching company, after a successful career in Information Technology. He observed that leaders who had excelled with tasks and were promoted into "people" leadership positions struggled.

This resulted in The Leadership Journey™, a 12 session program that has graduated thousands of leaders of all levels, and positions alumni to become Certified Professional Leaders.

Mike received his MBA from Nova Southeastern University, is a member of SHRM, ICF, ACEC and is a MEECO certified Executive Coach who resides by the ocean in Ft. Lauderdale.

Jan Mayer-Rodriguez is Vice President of Operations. Prior to PeopleTek™ Jan had a 27 year career with American Express that focused on customer and employee satisfaction levels, delivering superior products, and building effective cross team behaviors.

A native Michigander, Jan graduated from Eastern Michigan University with Bachelor of Science degrees in Criminal Justice and Sociology and now resides in Tennesee.

Discover The Magic

TWELVE REASONS WHY PEOPLETEK'S LEADERSHIP JOURNEY HAS HELPED THOUSANDS BECOME MORE EFFECTIVE LEADERS

AMPLIFIED AWARENESS

Proven to significantly amplify levels of self-awareness, and heighten leaders' awareness of others' styles and preferences.

COMMUNICATION STYLES

Understand why varied approaches and styles are effective in different situations. Communicate with others in their preferred styles to improve results and enhance relationships.

THE POWER OF MAGIC DUST

It's a science, but it works like magic to validate your strengths, preferred styles and preferences, and uncover areas you need to develop most.

VISIONARY CLARITY

Discover the power of having clearly-defined roles, responsibilities, and desired results. Do things with purpose... and never by accident.

VMGM = B

Learn the secrets behind why your Vision, Mission, Goals and Measures must be supported by your Behaviors, and tracked, documented, and shared with others.

ACCOUNTABILITY. ACCOUNTABILITY. ACCOUNTABILITY.

We must not only hold ourselves accountable, we should encourage others to do so, and lead by example.

Discover The Magic

TWELVE REASONS WHY PEOPLETEK'S LEADERSHIP JOURNEY HAS HELPED THOUSANDS BECOME MORE EFFECTIVE LEADERS

PeopleTek

COMPASS

LEADERSHIP
Journey

 **HONORING AND
EMBRACING CONFLICT**

Research clearly shows that honoring conflict is both healthy and necessary. It has also been linked to an increase in inspiration, innovative thinking, and collaboration.

 **FEEDBACK FEEDS
YOUR EFFECTIVENESS**

Your ability to give and receive feedback is critical to your success. The more we understand how others see us, the deeper we understand ourselves.

 **THE KEY TO
INFLUENCING OTHERS**

How you present yourself dramatically affects your ability to influence others; hence, we all have the ability to be effective leaders!

 **INSPIRATION
FUELS SUCCESS**

Individuals feel valued when inspired by others to stretch beyond their limits.

 **AUTHENTIC, LASTING
RELATIONSHIPS**

It's more than just accomplishing a task. An effective leader builds and maintains authentic, lasting relationships.

 **CONTINUAL LEARNING
(TRUE NORTH)**

Effective leaders commit to continual learning; it's a process, not an event. In an AI-driven world, continual learning is more important than ever before.

Self Discovery

RATE YOUR EFFECTIVENESS IN EACH OF THE SKILLS BELOW.

Awareness :: Skills and behaviors of self

1 = Poor; 10 = Superb

1	2	3	4	5	6	7	8	9	10

Awareness :: Skills and behaviors of others

1	2	3	4	5	6	7	8	9	10

Magic Dust :: Know and leverage your strengths

1	2	3	4	5	6	7	8	9	10

Vision/Mission/Goals :: ALL your behaviors support them

1	2	3	4	5	6	7	8	9	10

Communication :: Your message is accurately interpreted

1	2	3	4	5	6	7	8	9	10

Clarity :: Of roles, responsibilities, and desired results

1	2	3	4	5	6	7	8	9	10

Accountability :: For self

1	2	3	4	5	6	7	8	9	10

Conflict :: Manage and address conflict

1	2	3	4	5	6	7	8	9	10

Influence :: How you present yourself to others

1	2	3	4	5	6	7	8	9	10

Relationships :: Build and maintain lasting relationships

1	2	3	4	5	6	7	8	9	10

Feedback :: Give and receive feedback

1	2	3	4	5	6	7	8	9	10

Inspiration :: Empower and stretch others

1	2	3	4	5	6	7	8	9	10

Continual Learning :: Embrace and lead change

1	2	3	4	5	6	7	8	9	10

Self Discovery

PEOPLETEK'S LEADERSHIP JOURNEY BUILDS SKILLS AND ABILITIES

IDENTIFY YOUR STRENGTHS • TARGET DEVELOPMENT AREAS • IDENTIFY WHO CAN HELP

TAKE ACTION!

EXISTING STRENGTHS (RATED 8-10)

AREAS TO DEVELOP

WHO CAN HELP

NEXT STEPS AND TIMING

Printed in the United States
By Bookmasters